AF445292

ABC
DINOSAURS

copyright © Thomasine Media 2022

Images belong to their respective owners and are licensed for this publication

Book created by P.G. Hibbert

ISBN 979-8-9872958-3-0

ABC DINOSAURS

Learn the alphabet with Dinosaurs!

P.G. Hibbert

Ankylosaurus

B

Brontosaurus

Carnotaurus

Dilophosaurus

Elasmosaurus

Family

Gallimimus

Hadrosaurus

Iguanodon

Jobaria

Kentrosaurus

Lambeosaurus

Mosasaurus

Nedoceratops

Oviraptor

P

Pteradactyl

Quaesitosaurus

Rebbachisaurus

Spinosaurus

T

Tyrannosaurus Rex

Utahraptor

V

Velociraptor

Wannanosaurus

Xenoceratops

Yinlong

Zalmoxes

www.ingramcontent.com/pod-product-compliance
Lightning Source LLC
Chambersburg PA
CBHW081936120726
47997CB00010B/3154